Pebble® Plus

ZOO ANIMAL MYSTERIES

A Cool Caper

by Martha E. H. Rustad

Consulting Editor: Gail Saunder-Smith, PhD

Consultant: Jackie Gai, DVM
Zoo and Exotic Animal Consultant

CAPSTONE PRESS
a capstone imprint

Pebble Plus is published by Capstone Press,
151 Good Counsel Drive, P.O. Box 669, Mankato, Minnesota 56002.
www.capstonepub.com

032010
005740CGF10

Books published by Capstone Press are manufactured with paper containing at least 10 percent
post-consumer waste.

Library of Congress Cataloging-in-Publication Data
Rustad, Martha E. H. (Martha Elizabeth Hillman), 1975–
   A Cool Caper : a zoo animal mystery / by Martha E.H. Rustad.
       p. cm. — (Pebble plus. Zoo animal mysteries)
   Includes bibliographical references and index.
   Summary: "Simple text and full-color photographs present a mystery zoo animal, one feature at a time, until its identity
is revealed"— Provided by publisher.
   ISBN 978-1-4296-4498-3 (library binding)
   1. Adélie penguin—Juvenile literature. I. Title. II. Series.

QL696.S473R87 2011
598.47—dc22   2010001351

Editorial Credits
Jenny Marks, editor; Heidi Thompson, designer; Svetlana Zhurkin, media researcher; Eric Manske, production specialist

Photo Credits
Alamy/blickwinkel, 19
AnimalsAnimals/Mark Chappell, 9
iStockphoto/Brandon Laufenberg, cover
Peter Arnold/Biosphoto/Guillaume Bouteloup, 17
Photolibrary/Ted Mead, 14–15
Seapics/Ingrid Visser, 11; Mark Jones, 13
Shutterstock/Armin Rose, 4–5; Gen Productions, 7; wcpmedia, 20–21

Note to Parents and Teachers

The Zoo Animal Mysteries set supports national science standards related to life science.
This book describes and illustrates Adélie penguins. The images support early readers in
understanding the text. The repetition of words and phrases helps early readers learn new
words. This book also introduces early readers to subject-specific vocabulary words, which are
defined in the Glossary section. Early readers may need assistance to read some words and to
use the Table of Contents, Glossary, Read More, Internet Sites, and Index sections of the book.

Table of Contents

It's a Mystery

This book is full of clues

about a mystery zoo animal.

And that animal is me!

Can you guess what I am?

Here's your first clue:

In the wild, you'll find me

on and around icy Antarctica.

Antarctica

Where I Live

My Life and Kids

My winters are spent

swimming in icy water.

I dive underwater to catch prey.

When I need to rest,

I lie on a floating iceberg.

In spring, my flock and I

gather on rocky beaches.

My mate and I build a nest

out of pebbles.

Both of us care for our eggs.

Our chicks hatch in one month.

They have dark, soft feathers
called down.

We feed our chicks
and keep them warm.

Body Parts

My sharp beak catches

fish, squid, and krill to eat.

I also use my beak

to pick up rocks

when I build a nest.

I waddle on my feet

from my nest to the ocean.

Sliding on my belly

is sometimes faster.

My feet push me along.

Black and white feathers

cover my body.

My short, waterproof

feathers keep me warm.

I molt once each year.

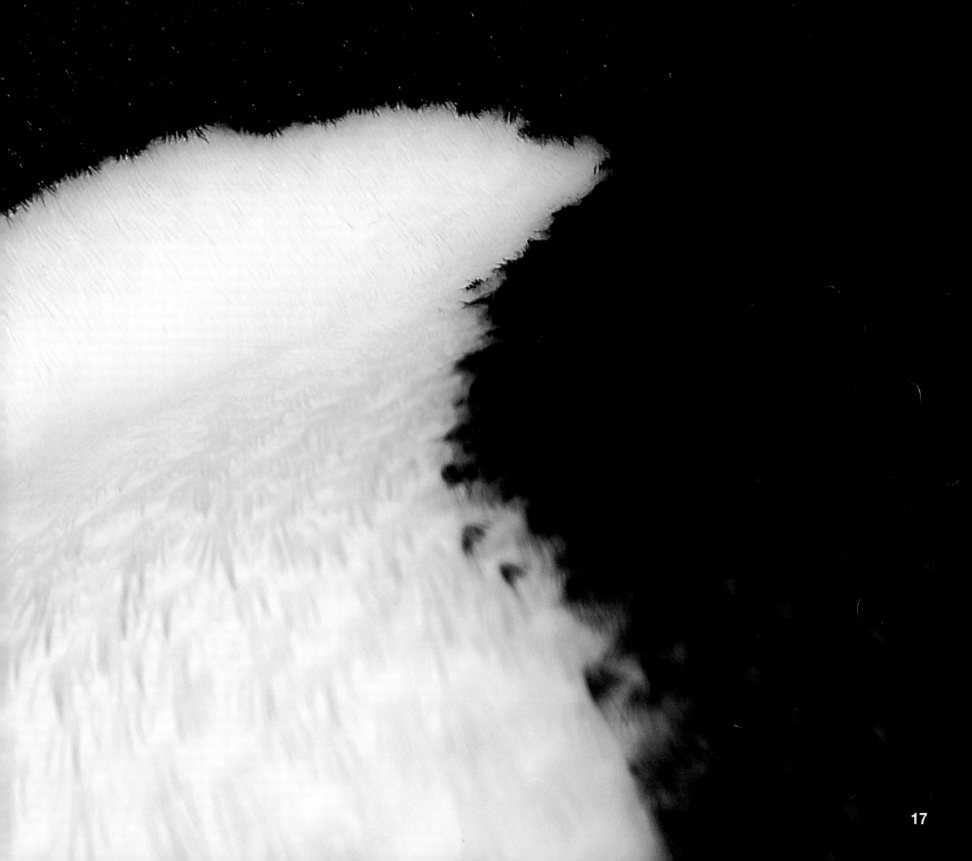

I have wings but cannot fly.

My wings are flippers

that help me swim.

Have you guessed

what I am?

19

Mystery Solved!

I'm an Adélie penguin!

This zoo mystery is solved.

Glossary

down—the soft feathers of a young penguin

flipper—a flat limb with bones on a sea animal; penguins use their wings as flippers

flock—a group of the same kind of birds

iceberg—a huge piece of ice that floats in the ocean

krill—a tiny, shrimplike animal that lives in the ocean; penguins eat krill

mate—one of a pair of animals

molt—to lose old feathers and grow new ones

prey—an animal hunted by another animal for food

waddle—to walk with short steps while moving from side to side

Read More

Gallagher, Debbie. *Penguins.* Zoo Animals.
New York: Marshall Cavendish Benchmark, 2010.

Kudela, Katy R. *The Pebble First Guide to Penguins.*
Pebble First Guides. Mankato, Minn.: Capstone
Press, 2009.

Sexton, Colleen A. *The Life Cycle of a Penguin.*
Blastoff! Readers: Life Cycles. Minneapolis: Bellwether
Media, 2010.

Internet Sites

FactHound offers a safe, fun way to find Internet sites
related to this book. All of the sites on FactHound have
been researched by our staff.

Here's all you do:

Visit *www.facthound.com*

Type in this code: 9781429644983

Index

Word Count: 201

Grade: 1

Early-Intervention Level: 15